ما لو

PARANORMAL
SEEKERS™

TRACKING
THE LOCH NESS
MONSTER

**JENNA VALE AND
MARTIN DELRIO**

rosen publishing's
**rosen
central**®

New York

Published in 2019 by The Rosen Publishing Group, Inc.
29 East 21st Street, New York, NY 10010

Copyright © 2019 by The Rosen Publishing Group, Inc.

First Edition

Library of Congress Cataloging-in-Publication Data

Names: Vale, Jenna, author. | Delrio, Martin, author.
Title: Tracking the Loch Ness Monster / Jenna Vale and Martin Delrio.
Description: New York : Rosen Publishing, 2019. | Series: Paranormal seekers | Includes bibliographical references and index. | Audience: Grades 5–8.
Identifiers: LCCN 2018015264| ISBN 9781508185741 (library bound) | ISBN 9781508185734 (pbk.)
Subjects: LCSH: Loch Ness monster—Juvenile literature.
Classification: LCC QL89.2.L6 V35 2018 | DDC 001.944—dc23
LC record available at https://lccn.loc.gov/2018015264

Manufactured in the United States of America

CONTENTS

INTRODUCTION

One of the deepest lakes in Great Britain has unusual physical features, draws tourists from all over the world, and hosts the best-known underwater legend apart from Atlantis. Loch Ness is situated in the Scottish Highlands, and because of its sheer volume, it's incredibly difficult to search thoroughly for any strange lifeforms. Even so, there have been claims of a mysterious creature in the loch for centuries.

From 1933 on, there have been serious efforts to find out just what is lurking in these deep waters. The loch measures 24 miles (38.6 kilometers) long yet only about 1 mile (1.6 km) wide. As for how deep it is, in January 2016, new depths seemed to be found using sonar, which uncovered a crevice that reached 889 feet (270.9 meters) deep. Discovered by a man named Keith Stewart, the area came to be known as "Keith's Abyss." What's more, Keith saw something else: a long object with a hump lying at the bottom of the trench. Stewart alleged the object was there during one scan, but not during the next one he did, leading him to believe it was perhaps the legendary Loch Ness monster itself. However, a later scan conducted by a sonar-equipped underwater drone found Keith's scans to be inaccurate, so the deepest point of Loch Ness is still officially 754 feet (230 m).

Accurate sonar readings have been difficult to record due to the loch's varying temperatures and steep stone

So many sightings of a huge, mysterious sea monster have been reported in Loch Ness that even search parties such as the one shown here have been sent out over the years in order to find traces of the mythical beast.

sides. These factors, on top of the fact that objects such as driftwood float on the water's surface, make it hard to discern exactly what objects are being picked up by echosounders, so the Loch Ness monster, or "Nessie," cannot definitively be ruled out.

The lack of proof—and disproof—may be the number-one reason why the legend still lives in the public consciousness: the curiosity is never satisfied. Mysterious creatures, or cryptids, such as Nessie, intrigue people and awaken any number of reasons for them to consider taking up the search. They might just want to believe such a fantastic creature is real, or their motives might be scientific or skeptical. At the heart of the matter is the fact that there are still things humanity has not discovered about the world, and there is nothing more human than the quest for knowledge.

People engage with legends in different ways. In this particular case concerning the Scottish loch, there have been famous photographs, inexplicable sightings as well as staged ones, Hollywood appearances, and group efforts to find evidence. With so many conflicting reports and odd features coexisting in one lake, it's easy to see how people might believe there is more to Loch Ness than meets the eye.

CHAPTER ONE

WHY LOCH NESS?

The story of the Loch Ness monster begins more than fourteen hundred years ago, in 565 CE. In that year, the Irish missionary Saint Columba had a dramatic encounter with a water monster. Columba's biographer, Saint Adamnan, tells the story in thrilling detail. Columba needed to cross the River Ness, and when he came upon people burying a man who had supposedly been bitten by the monster in the river, Columba had one of his companions swim across the river. The monster was far from satisfied after its first victim, and rose to strike the companion. Columba raised his hand and commanded the monster to stop. Adamnan writes, "Then at the voice of the saint, the monster was terrified, and fled more quickly than if it had been pulled back with ropes."

Adamnan's story is interesting—but is it true? Adamnan himself undoubtedly believed it. But Adamnan wrote his *Life of St. Columba* over a century after Saint Columba's supposed meeting with the lake (or river) monster.

Also, the monster seen by Saint Columba is different in at least two ways from the creature described in modern reports. Saint Columba's monster makes "an awful roar," and it is a killer. The modern Loch Ness monster, on the other hand, makes no sounds and doesn't attack people. All that the story really reveals is that reports of a water monster near Loch Ness go back at least as far as the sixth century.

IN MURKY WATERS

Legends of water monsters are well known in the Highlands of Scotland. The kelpie, also known as the water horse, was a creature that lived in and about the lochs. The name "water horse" came from its habit of taking the appearance of a fine horse standing saddled and bridled by the roadside. Unfortunate travelers who tried to ride this horse would find themselves stuck on its back, unable to let loose of the reins, as the creature plunged headlong into the nearby loch. Like many tales of fantastic creatures, the story of the kelpie has an element of the cautionary tale, warning travelers from engaging with strange people or beasts, and warning children against playing on the dangerous, slippery shores of the lochs.

Over time, the stories about the Highland water horses grew less fantastical and more realistic. Gone were the enchanted bridles and the death plunges, but from time to time the occasional sighting of an unusual animal would still be reported in the local press.

Stories of kelpies are associated with many of the lochs and other bodies of water in Scotland. These spirits typically appear in the form of a horse, but they can change into human form as well.

For example, in 1802, a man named Alexander MacDonald saw a large stubby-legged animal surface and propel itself to within 50 yards (45 m) of where he stood on the shore of the loch. In 1880 another Mac-Donald—named Duncan this time—dove into the loch near Fort Augustus to inspect the keel of a wrecked ship. While he was down there he saw an animal like a huge frog lying on an underwater shelf of rock. And in 1926, the *Inverness Courier* reported that a Simon McGarry of Invergarry saw the gulls rise screaming into the air above the loch, and a creature emerge. "Before my eyes, something like an upturned boat rose from the depths, and I can still see the water cascading down its sides. Just as suddenly, though, it sank out of sight."

OTHER LEGENDARY WATER-DWELLING BEASTS

The mysteries of deep waters have mystified people for all of human history. Strange incidents, speculation, and developing folklore have resulted in stories of many kinds of beasts, from underwater monsters like the Leviathan to the many-headed Hydra.

The Leviathan is a sea serpent that comes from Jewish mythology. It's mentioned in the Hebrew Bible as a multi-headed serpent that glides through the sea and has eyes that emit a brilliant light. The Hydra, a dragonlike creature with many heads from Greek mythology, has appeared in legends and poems dating as far back as 700 BCE. As the famous legend goes, whenever one of the Hydra's heads was cut off, two would grow back in its place, making it a formidable monster indeed.

There have also been accounts and legends of other sea serpents, demonic whales, colossal walruses and octopuses, and even a fish that looks like a man in monk's robes, appropriately referred to as the "sea monk." The sea monk was found off the coast of Zealand, a Danish island, in 1546. In centuries since, scientists have speculated that the sea monk was actually a giant squid, a walrus, or perhaps an angelshark.

The oarfish is another real sea creature that might account for some legends: it's a tropical eel-like creature that lives in deep water and can reach a length of about 30.5 feet (9 m)—it would certainly look like a mysterious sea serpent!

The legendary Hydra lurked in the gloomy marshes near the Greek city of Árgos. One of its heads was also immortal.

THE LOCH'S FORMATION

Before any peculiar creatures could possibly call Loch Ness home, it of course had to form. Four hundred million years ago, in what would someday become the Scottish Highlands, part of the Caledonian Mountains slid more than 60 miles (96 km) to the south. The fault line left a rift valley a mile (1.61 km) wide that still runs all the way across Scotland, from the North Sea to the Atlantic Ocean. This valley is Glen Mor, the Great Glen. Loch Ness lies in the northeastern-most portion of the Great Glen.

Over time the continents cracked apart and drifted. During the Age of Dinosaurs, long-necked plesiosaurs swam in the shallow seas that covered much of North America and Europe. Mammals arose, dinosaurs died off, the climate grew colder, and eventually ice sheets spread over much of the world.

During the Ice Age, glaciers covered the Scottish Highlands with a layer of ice up to 4,000 feet (1,219 m) deep. The ice pressed down on the land and caused the rock to sink beneath sea level. As the ice melted, the land rose. The portion of the rift valley that would become Loch Ness was an arm of the sea. The rising land, the falling sea level, and the melting glaciers worked together to cut off the loch from the ocean and replace the salt water with fresh water. The surface of the loch is now about 52 feet (15.8 m) above sea level.

Humans came into the Great Glen area around 6,000 years ago. The first settlers were the Picts, whose name comes from the Latin *Picti*, or "painted people," a nickname the Romans gave them because of their fondness for tattoos and body paint.

Loch Ness today is the largest of a series of glacial lakes running along the fault line of the Great Glen from Inverness to Fort William. The Loch Ness holds the greatest volume of fresh water in Great Britain, with steep sides and a lakebed of soft, level mud. The rock walls of the loch extend below the mud in a V shape, and may go down as far as 900 feet (274.3 m). Not counting the mud and whatever lies below it, Loch Ness is the second-deepest lake in the British Isles (second only to

The Pict tribes made up the biggest kingdom in Dark Age Scotland. In addition to their body art, they carved designs into stones, metalwork, and even bones. Pictish stones can still be found around Scotland today.

Loch Morar, which is 1,017 feet (310 m) deep at its deepest point), and the third-deepest lake in Europe. The River Ness, about 7 miles (11 km) long, drains the loch into the sea at Beauly Firth. The Highland city of Inverness is located on the river, between Loch Ness and the sea.

The waters of Loch Ness are dark and cold, murky with particles of peat moss washed in by the streams that feed the loch. The sun warms the upper levels of the loch, down to about 150 feet (45.7 m). Below 150 feet the water maintains a constant temperature near 45 degrees Fahrenheit (7.2° Celsius). The loch never freezes over even in the coldest Highland winters.

SHAPING THE MONSTER

Is there a large animal in Loch Ness? The monster usually takes one of three forms. The first and most common is the moving wake, a pattern of waves in the water hinting at the presence of something large swimming just beneath. The second is a humped body, either moving or stationary, rising above the water. The third, and rarest, form is a long neck with a small head.

But could an undiscovered animal as large as the Loch Ness monster possibly exist? The answer is yes. Animals previously unknown to science have been found more than once in the past hundred years. For instance, there's the megamouth shark (*Megachasma pelagios*), a creature 15 feet (4.6 m) long and weighing nearly a ton. The first specimen was discovered on November 15, 1976, when it was found entangled in the drag anchor of a US Navy ship. The new creature wasn't described scientifically until 1983. Twelve years after the first sighting, only three specimens had been found. Since that time, it's estimated there have been over a hundred sightings. The megamouth remains the only species in its genus, and the only genus in its order.

More recently there's the saola, a bovine resembling an antelope that was discovered in Southeast Asia in 1992. Local inhabitants, of course, had always known about the animal, but mainstream science hadn't gotten the word until then. Only four of them have been seen by scientists since then, so they are considered to be

The megamouth shark's mouth and jaw are much larger than its abdomen. It eats plankton like a whale, and its lips are believed to be bioluminescent to help it attract prey in the deep sea.

critically endangered. Because of their appearance and rarity, they're often referred to as the Asian unicorn. Other animals once thought to be legendary have been proven to exist within the last hundred years, too: the giant panda, the giant squid, and the Kodiak bear.

Sometimes creatures thought to have vanished long ago are rediscovered as well. The coelacanth, an ancient fish, was known only from the fossil record. Scientists thought the species had died out some four hundred million years ago. Then, in 1938, a fisherman caught a coelacanth off the coast of Africa. A second one turned up in 1952, and others have been seen since.

Whether or not Nessie might be a new animal or an old one waiting to be rediscovered, there is no reason to rule out its existence just yet. On the subject of the Loch Ness monster, the Smithsonian Institution says, "Even though most scientists believe the likelihood of a monster is small, they keep an open mind as scientists should and wait for concrete proof in the form of skeletal evidence or the actual capture of such a creature." Until then, observers on the shore will keep on looking for a rippled wake, or a humped back, or a long-necked creature rising out of the depths—and the waters of Loch Ness will keep their secrets.

CHAPTER TWO

RISING FROM THE LAKEBED

When it comes to the Loch Ness monster, what do the reported sightings indicate? To consider the creature, the history of people's accounts must be considered carefully. On July 22, 1930, for example, three young men from Inverness were fishing from a boat near Dores. They sighted a disturbance in the water that commenced about 600 yards (548.6 m) away from them, moved toward them until it came to within 300 yards (274 m), with a part protruding from the water being 20 feet (6 m) long by 3 feet (.9 m) high. The report was alarming, and the years that followed produced similar accounts.

1933: THE YEAR OF NESSIE

The year of 1933 in particular was rife with sightings. On April 14, 1933, the Mackays were driving along the side of Loch Ness on the new road from Inverness. Near the town of Abriachan, Mrs. Mackay spotted "an enormous animal rolling and plunging" in the center of the loch.

The *Daily Express*, a Glasgow newspaper, reported on June 9, 1933: "Mystery fish in Scottish loch. Monster reported at Fort Augustus. A monster fish which for years has been somewhat of a mystery in Loch Ness was reported to have been seen yesterday at Fort Augustus."

On July 22, 1933, a man named George Spicer and his wife reported the first sighting of the Loch Ness monster on land. They said the animal was limbless, and its body was about 4 to 5 feet (1.2–1.5 m) high and perhaps 25 feet (8 m) long. Its neck was slightly thicker than an elephant's trunk and measured as long as 10 to 12 feet (3–4 m), which was also the width of the road on which they were traveling. It was gray and moved in a series of jerks and lurches, resembling a giant snail with a long neck.

On October 23, 1933, the London *Daily Mail* reported from Scotland: "In Inverness, the Highland Capital, there is one topic of conversation—'the beast' as by one accord everybody dubs the uncanny denizen of the loch by this sinister title. Some think the loch harbors a survivor of some prehistoric creature that may have been

There are more than thirty thousand lochs in Scotland for visitors to see, and some people have speculated that many of the monster sightings have been reported in order to increase tourism for the Loch Ness area.

released from the earth's recesses by the great blasting operations required for the making of the new Inverness-Glasgow motor road."

On October 29, 1933, E. G. Boulenger, the director of the aquarium at the London Zoo, sounded a word of caution: "The case of the Monster in Loch Ness is worthy of our consideration if only because it presents a striking example of mass hallucination."

On November 13, 1933, the government became involved. Sir Murdoch MacDonald, who represented Inverness-shire in Parliament, wrote to the Secretary of State for Scotland:

> As no doubt you are aware, some animal or fish of an unusual kind has found its way into Loch Ness. I think I can say the evidence of its presence can be taken as undoubted. Far too many people have seen something abnormal to question its existence. So far, there has been no indication of its being a harmful animal or fish, and until somebody states the genus to which it belongs, I do hope you can authorise the police in the district to prevent pothunters deliberately looking for it.

But the tales of the Loch Ness monster proved to be more than just a seven-day-wonder and a silly-season newspaper flash. Interest has endured over the years: there is even a Loch Ness Monster Sightings Register that counts itself as the official log of monster sightings. By their records, there have been over a thousand recorded sightings to date. They keep photos and descriptions of the sightings cataloged by year, with eleven sightings reported in 2017 alone. The register also provides information on what is not considered a sighting, which is important because of the loch's size and conditions. For example, an observer standing at the waterline and looking across the loch will find that the opposite shore is halfway to the horizon. Looking lengthwise down the loch, the same observer would not be able to see the far end at all.

Weather conditions at the loch are extreme, too. Between 1920 and 1950, the weather station at Fort Augustus reported fewer sunny days than any other station in Britain. The wind howls up the Great Glen, whipping the surface of the loch to foam where a moment before the water had been still and glassy. Observation is even trickier during twilight, and the high northern latitude of Scotland produces long periods of twilight.

Making observations across open water is difficult at best. Estimating size and distance is hard without familiar objects near the unknown to provide a scale. Open water is also prone to mirage conditions. A floating log, a bird, a distant boat, a wind-blown wave, a deer swimming in the loch—any of these things, seen under the right lighting conditions, could be misinterpreted as a fabulous monster. Furthermore, human memories are fallible. People see what they want to see and remember what they want to remember.

SKEPTICS ON THE SCENE

Stories are one thing, but even the first photographic "evidence" of the monster did not seem too promising, though many saw it as indisputable proof at the time. On November 12, 1933, a Highlander named Hugh Gray was walking along the river near the village of Foyers when he saw a creature rolling around in the water. He was carrying a camera, and he managed to photograph it. Some people who look at the photo see the head of a dog with a stick in its mouth, swimming toward the camera. Others see an otter or a swan. In any case, it is worth noting that Gray was walking his Labrador retriever on the day he took the photograph.

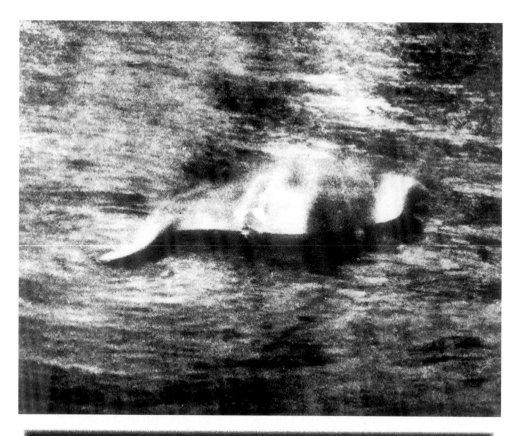

Hugh Gray's photo made quite a splash when it was revealed in late 1933. Unfortunately, the blurred version seen here was the best result developed from Gray's film, and the original negative has been lost.

Matters were not helped when the next piece of hard evidence turned out to be a provable hoax. The London *Daily Mail* hired a professional big-game hunter to go to Loch Ness and bring back evidence of the creature's existence. The hunter, Marmaduke "Duke" Wetherall, arrived in mid-December of 1933. Within a few days Wetherall had found mysterious footprints on the shores of the loch. He dutifully made a plaster cast and sent it back to London for identification, all amidst great publicity. And amid great publicity came the answer, issued from the British Museum of Natural History on January 4, 1934: the footprints were all made by the right rear foot of a female hippopotamus. Stuffed. Someone had apparently used a hippopotamus-foot umbrella stand to create the "monster" footprints, and Wetherall had fallen for it.

Instantly, the Loch Ness monster became a laughing-stock that no legitimate scientist could touch and come away from with his reputation intact. Forty years later, when the Academy of Applied Science launched an expedition to the loch in an attempt to take underwater photos of the creature, it would be mocked by the comic strip "Doonesbury" as "the Academy of Implied Science." Wetherall stated that in his opinion the loch contained nothing more than a large gray seal. The publicity started to fade.

PLOT TWIST

Then came April 1934. On the nineteenth of that month, R. K. Wilson, a respected London surgeon, was on holiday in Scotland. Around 7:00 in the morning, Wilson

ANALYZING PHOTOGRAPHS

When arguing for the existence of the Loch Ness monster, photos should provide some of the most compelling evidence. But can photographs be taken at face value? That is, are they real? In the case of Hugh Gray's photo, it is, at best, a blurry shot of something unidentifiable. There are no foreground objects with which to make a size comparison. Gray estimated the object to be 200 yards (182.8 m) away. An ordinary camera is hard-pressed to take detailed photos at that range. Gray stated that the object was obscured by spray, that it was dark gray in color, and that it stood 3 to 4 feet (.9 to 1.2 m) out of the water. He took five shots with his camera, then went home.

And there his camera, with what could be astounding pictures inside, lay untouched for two weeks. The most charitable interpretation of this delay is the one Gray himself gives—he was afraid that nothing would appear on the film, and that he would be kidded by his fellow workers. When the film was at last developed, four of the five shots showed nothing, and the fifth showed what seemed to be a creature with its head underwater, the tail farthest from the photographer.

stopped about 2 miles (3 km) north of Invermoriston. Wilson was a few yards (2.7 m) down the slope and facing the loch when, he said:

Most alleged photos of the monster show part of a creature that could look like the plesiosaur depicted here. Many people believe Nessie might be a surviving plesiosaur, and it is often portrayed as one.

I noticed a considerable commotion on the surface some distance out from the shore, perhaps two or three hundred yards [274 meters] out. I watched it for perhaps a minute or so and saw something break the surface. My friend shouted: "My God, it's the Monster!"

Wilson then stated:

I ran the few yards to the car and got the camera and then went down and along the steep bank for about fifty yards to where my friend was and got the camera focused on something which was moving through the water. I could not say what this object was as I was far too busy managing the camera in my amateurish way.

Wilson took four photos, which he brought to be developed that same day in Inverness. The pictures came back that afternoon. The first two were blank; the third showed what appeared to be a head and neck rising above the water. The fourth showed the creature sinking back into the loch.

That third, best-known photo is certainly startling. If this is indeed the head and neck of a creature extending 4 feet (1.2 m) above the surface of the loch, it resembles nothing so much as a plesiosaur, a carnivorous aquatic reptile thought to have become extinct some sixty-five million years ago.

CHAPTER THREE

"WE'LL GIVE THEM THEIR MONSTER!"

Just as Hugh Gray's picture proved problematic, so too did Wilson's. When someone photographs an unknown object, it's essential that they include objects of known size in the foreground of the shot, otherwise the exact size of the unknown can't be determined. In the case of Wilson's photo, rather than seeing a large object far off the shore, some people saw a small object close by: a water bird, the tail of a diving otter, or a floating log with a root sticking above the water. Wilson sold the head-and-neck picture to the *Daily Mail* when he returned to London and created an instant sensation. Some people were convinced of the authenticity of "the Surgeon's Photo," but others were skeptical.

One objection is that while Wilson said the thing he photographed was moving, the ripples on the water show it to be stationary. Perhaps, some say, it was moving, but had stopped by the time he got his camera to his eye. Perhaps, others suggest, it was never moving at all.

The second photo, the one the newspaper didn't run, is of far poorer quality than the famous shot. Neverthe-

The Surgeon's Photo is still associated with Nessie but generally as a hoax rather than proof. The "monster" in the photo was supposedly staged using a toy submarine with an added plastic head and neck!

less, it has some interesting features. One is that the angle between the "head" and the "neck" of the object has changed.

SUSPECTING A HOAX

On March 13, 1994, the London *Sunday Telegraph* ran a story claiming the famous photo was actually of an 18-inch (45.7 cm) model, and that Wilson had not taken the photos himself, but had allowed his name and reputation to be used for the occasion. According to the *Sunday Telegraph*, a man named Christian Spurling had confessed to perpetrating a hoax sixty years before at the urging of his stepfather—none other than "Duke" Wetherall, the big-game hunter who had himself been fooled by the dried hippo foot in 1933.

Across the pond, *New York Times* reporter John Darnton wrote on March 20, 1994, that Wetherell had planned to get back at those who disgraced him, telling his then twenty-one-year-old son, Ian, "We'll give them their monster!" Ian pulled his step-brother, Christian Spurling, into the plan, and the Surgeon's Photo plot was born.

By the time Spurling told his story, every-one else supposedly involved in the hoax was dead. And by the time the story was printed, Spurling himself was dead at the age of ninety. All anyone can say for certain, therefore, is that either Spurling was fibbing, or that Wilson was.

THE SEARCH INTENSIFIES

The history of the Loch Ness monster continued after R. K. Wilson sold his picture to the *Daily Mail.* In the summer of 1934, Sir Edward Mountain, a gentleman described as "an enthusiastic angler," rented Beaufort Castle on Loch Ness and spent the month of July hunting for evidence of a creature. He hired twenty men and posted them a mile or so apart down the 24-mile (38.6 km) length of the loch. Each man had binoculars and a camera, and watched from 8 a.m. to 6 p.m. The men reported back every night on what they had seen. Sir Edward marked each sighting on a map of the loch. In two weeks of good weather, the watchers claimed to have sighted what could be a creature no fewer than twenty-one times and took five photos. Then bad weather set in, and the sightings stopped. The five photos were

Beaufort Castle is a Baronial-style mansion. It was built in 1880 on the remains of Dounie Castle, with some of the original stonework incorporated into the new building, including the long wall beside it.

"disappointing," lacking even the detail of the London surgeon's photo. No conclusions could be drawn.

Sir Edward switched to one man with a movie camera and a telephoto lens. This eventually yielded movie footage of something later identified by zoologists as a large

THE SCIENTIFIC APPROACH

Science works, first, by collecting the available information, or data, about the thing being studied. Second, scientists take this information and try to come up with a hypothesis that explains how the data fits together. Third, they devise experiments to test those hypotheses. Once a hypothesis is verified by the experimental method, it becomes a theory.

Along the way there are several general principles. One is called Occam's razor, after William of Occam, a medieval monk and early scientist who said, "Logical entities should not be multiplied unnecessarily." Another way of putting that is, "If you have two competing theories that make exactly the same predictions, the one that is simpler is the better one."

The least complex theory may still be quite complex. As Albert Einstein put it, "Everything should be made as simple as possible, but not simpler."

Given two hypotheses, one that "the sightings of unidentified objects in Loch Ness are caused by unknown animals seen at great distances under bad light conditions" and the second that "the sightings of unidentified objects in Loch Ness are caused by floating logs seen at great distances under bad light conditions," the log explanation is simpler. It has already been proven, by other means, that there are floating logs in the loch.

Is there a reasonable way to prove Loch Ness (or, indeed, any body of water) is monster free? If a search fails to find any monsters, then perhaps the search was in the wrong location, at the wrong time, or using the wrong means. If one photo turns out to be a fake, that doesn't mean the next photo won't be real. If one observer is mistaken, that doesn't mean the next observer will be inaccurate.

Maybe one day the right photo, video, or sonar reading will reveal the Loch Ness monster and lead scientists to a creature they can study in the flesh. Until that time, the more that can be understood about the loch itself, the easier it will be to separate the hazy uncertainties from the objective truth.

seal, the same conclusion that Wetherall had reached earlier that year. Sir Edward's film has since been lost.

During World War II, the loch came under the control of the Royal Navy. The monster was forgotten. Then in 1951, a worker for the Forestry Commission named Lachlan Stuart saw what he first thought was a large motorboat speeding down the loch. Realizing that it was no motorboat, he grabbed a camera and took a photograph of a three-humped creature that he estimated to be about 57 feet (17.4 m) long from nose to tail.

A creature that might have such a shape is difficult to imagine. Some people see not one creature, but three in a pack traveling together. Others claim the photo is of three separate hay bales floating in the loch, and that Stuart was either mistaken or lying when he claimed he saw them move.

This image shows sonar readings for an area of Loch Ness's lake floor. People have tried documenting Loch Ness with sonar for decades, but a complete picture has yet to be formed.

There matters might have stood, but new evidence from another source turned up. On December 2, 1954, a fishing boat named *Rival III* out of Peterhead was passing down the loch when something unusual turned up on the echosounder. The device showed an object off Urquhart Bay, 480 feet (146.3 m) down, 120 feet (36.5 m) above the bottom of the loch. Experts who later examined the trace stated the echo wasn't the result of a mechanical malfunction from the machine, it hadn't been tampered with, and the object wasn't a water-logged tree or a shoal of fish.

CHAPTER FOUR

APPLYING SCIENCE TO THE SEARCH

Sonar continues to be used to search the loch, although with inconclusive or conflicting results, as in the case of Keith Stewart's "discovery" of an abyss, which only proved the necessity for independent verification. The water under the thermocline, which is a layer in bodies of water that has different temperatures above and below it, was once thought to be devoid of life; however, scientists now know it actually has an 80 percent oxygen saturation, and fish live there down to the bottom, where arctic char and lampreys swim in the blackness. But so far, no unknown animals have been brought to the surface.

Sea lampreys resemble eels, but these eerie creatures are more closely related to sharks! They are parasitic fish and are among the most primitive of vertebrate species.

SONAR IN THE LOCH

Some sonar searches have been disappointing. If identifying an animal from a blurry photograph is difficult, identifying one from a sonar echo is more so. The nearly vertical, parallel stone sides of Loch Ness, combined with the thermocline at 150 feet (45.7 m) down, produce difficult conditions for sonar operation. Sonar signals are bent or reflected when they hit a thermocline—submarines use this fact to hide from sonar searches.

In 1976, Christopher McGowan and Martin Klein searched the bottom of Loch Ness for the bones of a monster, using towed side-scan sonar. The system had found mastodon bones on the bottom of a lake in New Hampshire during a test run. But, while they found the remains of a crashed World War II aircraft in Loch Ness, and Pictish stone circles beneath the current waterline, no monster bones turned up. However, McGowan and Klein searched only the shallow areas of the loch.

In 1982, months of patrolling with scanning sonar produced forty hits on objects larger than the largest known fish, which could not be explained as false signals.

In 1987, Operation Deepscan was mounted. It consisted of nineteen boats sailing side by side, sweeping the loch from wall to wall with a curtain of sound. They sailed the long way down the loch, once each way, during the two-day search. Numerous strong sonar echoes "larger than a shark but smaller than a whale" were recorded. They all appeared to be moving, and many were below 150 feet (45.72 m). Yet problems abounded with this search, too. The sonar systems mounted on the boats interfered with each other, so they had to be set to their lowest power. At the end of the two-day sweep, all the expedition organizers had was a set of returns they couldn't identify at all, let alone suggest they belonged to a monster.

PHOTOGRAPHY ABOVE AND BELOW THE SURFACE

Observation and photography have continued to be a staple of the search at the loch's surface level. In 1960, a man named Tim Dinsdale took a movie of an unknown object in the loch. Some claim it was a motorboat seen at a great distance under poor lighting conditions, but Dinsdale claimed it was the hump of the monster. When the film was analyzed by Britain's Joint Air Reconnaissance Intelligence Center (JARIC) in 1966, the photographic experts said what the film showed was "probably an animate object." The video Dinsdale took can be viewed online.

Between the years 1962 and 1972, a group called the Loch Ness Phenomena Investigation Bureau ringed the loch with movie and still cameras fitted with telephoto lenses in an attempt to duplicate one or more of the classic monster photos. They were unable to do so. While they did get some photos of objects that could not be identified, they did not get any photos of objects that were definitely an unknown animal.

The Academy of Applied Sciences, an American group, launched an investigation of its own in the early 1970s, financed in part by the *New York Times* and the National Geographic Society. The expedition was led by Dr. Robert Rines. The equipment was designed by Harold "Doc" Edgerton, a professor at Massachusetts Institute of Technology (MIT) and the inventor of both strobe photography and side-scan sonar. When computer enhanced, the underwater photos they took seemed to show a large five-sided fin, and—in another photo—the head and neck of an unknown animal.

A team of experts from the British Museum of Natural History had this to say in November 1975:

> None of the photographs is sufficiently informative to establish the existence, far less the identity, of a large animal in the loch. To one of us it strongly suggested the head of a horse with a bridle, and others conceded this likeness when it was pointed out. The size limits are compatible with this explanation. On this interpretation, eyes, ears, noseband, and nostrils are visible, along with a less clear structure that could represent a neck. We believe that the image

Although there have been organizational changes over the years, members of the Loch Ness Phenomena Investigation Bureau have been conducting research on the loch and its alleged monster since 1962.

is too imprecise for us to argue that this does indeed represent a dead horse, but we equally believe that such an interpretation cannot be eliminated.

Unfortunately, the murky water of the loch made the underwater photos blurry and dim, and when others tried to computer enhance the original photos, they did not get the same results the academy did. Other investigations followed, with sonar, with surface and subsurface cameras, and even with small submarines. In the summer of 2000, a Swedish businessman asked for permission to cruise the loch with a specially modified crossbow in an attempt to get a skin sample from the unknown animal so DNA testing could show what it was. He was refused permission on the grounds that Scottish law forbids annoying livestock.

PROPOSALS APLENTY

Hypotheses abound. None of them are strong enough to make it up to the status of a theory. Assuming there is a creature, is it a mammal? Whales, seals, and giant otters have all been suggested— but sea mammals tend to be friendly and gregarious. They come up frequently for air, and on cold days their breath is visible. A family of whales spouting in the loch wouldn't remain mysterious for very long.

How about a reptile? The extinct plesiosaur looks like the Loch Ness monster of legend. The water in the loch is cold, but it never freezes, and the leatherback turtle, an ocean-dwelling reptile, lives in the waters off Scotland. But reptiles also need to come to the surface for air. Furthermore, it would be astonishing if a breeding population of plesiosaurs had survived undetected for sixty-five million years.

An amphibian, then? Amphibians' bodies sink when they die, and some

amphibians maintain gills all their lives. They might never need to come to the surface. Duncan MacDonald, the diver who saw something underwater in 1880, described what he saw as looking like a frog. But amphibians lay egg masses, and no such eggs have

Leatherback turtles are the largest turtles on the planet. They can grow up to 7 feet (2 m) long and weigh more than 2,000 pounds (907 kilograms).

DEBUNK IT!

What other explanations could be responsible for Nessie sightings? W. H. Lehn of the Department of Electrical Engineering at the University of Manitoba published an article, "Atmospheric Refraction and Lake Monsters," in *Science* magazine in 1979. He demonstrated that the refraction effect of layers of air at different temperatures could make logs and similar objects appear to stretch upward and transform into long-necked "monsters." Cold, deep Loch Ness is ideal for producing inversion layers of the kind Lehn suggests. But mirages don't alarm seabirds, and they don't create moving wakes that break on the shore. Other possibilities include:

- Minor earthquake activity. Loch Ness is in an active geologic fault.
- Equipment malfunction, or misinterpretation of recorded events, as is suspected in incidents such as the famous "Flipper Pictures" produced by the Academy of Applied Sciences.
- Collective mats of rotting vegetation, lifted by methane gas, which sink again after the gas bubbles burst into the air.

No such mats of vegetation have washed ashore, but there are two areas on the bottom of the loch—one off Fort Augustus, one off Urquhart Castle—that are known to produce methane.

been seen in the loch. How about a fish? Sturgeon can grow quite large and are certainly odd-looking creatures. But sturgeon don't have long necks or a tendency to come to the surface.

A large invertebrate, with no fixed body shape, could supply the wide variety of forms attributed to the Loch Ness monster. Some writers have suggested the long "neck" of the Loch Ness creature is a single tentacle of a giant squid, raised above the surface for a moment. One researcher suggested the Loch Ness creature is a Tully monster. Unfortunately, the Tully monster, like the plesiosaur, is long extinct—and its largest fossil is only a few centimeters long.

A LESSON IN BUOYANCY

Suppose there isn't a living creature at all? What else could people have been reporting? Boats, birds, and floating logs, seen at a great distance under poor lighting conditions, have all been suggested—but these explanations don't explain the close-up sightings.

Between 1969 and 2016, there actually was one confirmed monster in Loch Ness, but it wasn't a creature that was—or had ever been—alive. Indeed, it was a movie prop! The mock Loch Ness monster had been constructed for the movie *The Private Life of Sherlock Holmes* (1970), and been left there after filming. In 2016, a Norwegian company called Kongsberg Maritime dispatched an underwater robot in Loch Ness to conduct a sonar survey using multibeam sonar, and

A towering Nessie model glides towards Holmes's boat in this scene from *The Private Life of Sherlock Holmes*. Holmes comically listens to the loch's surface with a stethoscope to track the monster's approach.

the measurements, location, and shape indicated that it was in fact the movie prop.

Adrian Shine, who leads the Loch Ness Project, told BBC News Scotland in April 2016:

> The model was built with a neck and two humps and taken alongside a pier for filming of portions of the film in 1969. The director did not want the humps and asked that they be removed, despite warnings I suspect from the rest of the production that this would affect its buoyancy. And the inevitable happened. The model sank.

CHAPTER FIVE

THE DEPTHS OF POP CULTURE

One reason why the Loch Ness monster has captured the public's attention for so long is that it serves humanity's need to answer the unexplainable. Nearly every society is captured by a similar mystery. Whether it is the Loch Ness monster, Bigfoot, or UFOs, these unexplained phenomena give people a reason to seek the truth.

Indeed, humanity's interest in the monster may even have created more than what's really there, as in the case of the sunken movie prop. Speaking of movies, remember 1933, the year when reports of the Loch Ness monster spiked considerably? On April 7, 1933, the first *King Kong* movie was released, and it featured a terrifying sequence with a brontosaurus. Scientists now believe this dinosaur was a peaceful herbivore, or plant eater, but its name has Greek roots and roughly means "thunder lizard." In *King Kong*, the brontosaurus rises out of a body of water, its head pushing up atop a long neck. It wreaks havoc on a group of men exploring the island, and only after it runs onshore and its legs can be seen is it possible to identify the creature as the thunder lizard it's intended to portray. Chronologically speaking,

Although the brontosaurus is thought to have been a plant eater that was not threatened by most creatures, the thunder lizard of the original *King Kong* film definitely did not act that way!

it's interesting that the spike in Nessie sightings occurred after the movie's release. In any case, the Loch Ness monster has at least survived in popular culture, making appearances in literature, movies, and television.

NESSIE IN LITERATURE

The Loch Ness monster has appeared in literature for many years. Since the 1950s, there have been dozens of works written on the subject in magazines, newspapers, and books, including by such popular authors as J. K. Rowling, author of the *Harry Potter* series of young adult books. Interestingly, much of what is written is done so as nonfiction, even though the creature itself has still not yet been proven to exist.

In 1959, British mystery author and screenwriter Leslie Charteris penned the short story "The Convenient Monster," whose main character Simon Templar investigates an alleged monster attack. The roots of the story have many parallels with the story of the Loch Ness monster.

Though the actual Loch Ness monster doesn't appear in Charteris' story, there are many works of literature in which it does. In the 1977 book *The Mysterious Tadpole*, a boy receives a tadpole for his birthday and soon discovers that it is the offspring of the creature. In Susan Cooper's 1997 novel *The Boggart and the Monster*, the Loch Ness monster appears as a shape shifter. Finally, in J. K. Rowling's 2001 story *Fantastic Beasts and Where to Find Them*, the monster is actually discovered to be a supernatural water horse from Celtic folklore.

FILM APPEARANCES

Given its status as a cult icon, the Loch Ness monster is a perfect candidate for portrayal in cinema of all genres, including horror, thriller, suspense, and even comedy. Since the early twentieth century, virtually in the infancy of the cinema, up until today, the Loch Ness monster has been a star.

FOLKLORE AND WARNINGS

Before movies and television, the Loch Ness monster appeared in the public consciousness in the medium of the day: folklore. The monster was often associated with the legends of mystical lake creatures called kelpies. Kelpies were first described as being horselike and appeared out of the surface of the water. These tales served a distinct purpose to keep children away from and out of the lake.

More modern accounts of the Loch Ness monster made them appear more like plesiosaurs, an aquatic reptile that lived at the time of the dinosaurs, which were unknown at the time of the kelpie. Describing the monster as resembling plesiosaurs gives the monster a more realistic and credible identity. People are more apt to relate to a creature they have seen a likeness of and know existed in the past.

Whatever the origins, tales of the Loch Ness monster have been told for generations and will continue to be told. While the means of storytelling may change, the story itself remains the same.

The first picture to use the Loch Ness monster as a subject was the 1934 film *The Secret of the Loch*, which filmed a water snake and used special effects to turn it into the infamous character of the monster. Though this first portrayal in film was more or less straightforward, offering the literal storyline of the account of the creature, future filmmakers would grow considerably more creative in years to come.

In the second half of the century, "Nessie" appeared in the 1961 film *What a Whopper*, a British comedy written by Terry Nation, about a group of Englishmen who travel to the famous lake to fake sightings about the monster. This account of the monster reflected the grow-

The characters of *What a Whopper* encounter many fake models of Nessie on their quest for the perfect convincing hoax photograph, only to unexpectedly run into the real Loch Ness monster along the way.

ing intrigue with the mystery. On a certain level, *What a Whopper* quenched the public's thirst for an answer to the mystery. Going so far as to fake an account of a sighting, though fictional, offered a mild, and temporary, answer to the unanswered.

Using comedy to portray this mysterious and scary creature allows the public to see the Loch Ness monster in a softer light. Instead of approaching it, and any fearsome creature for that matter, as something to run away from, comedy allows people to embrace what is unknown or unknowable. This is similar to how people may use humor to talk about sensitive topics.

That being said, the monster's potential fierce side has also been explored in the horror genre, specifically in the 1981 film *The Loch Ness Horror*. The creature plays a central role in this film, going on a killing spree by feeding on unsuspecting swimmers. Adding to the monster's mystique, in the 1987 movie *Amazon Women on the Moon*, the Loch Ness monster was speculated to be the famous serial killer Jack the Ripper.

The Loch Ness monster has even appeared in animated movies, such as the 1992 picture *Freddie as F.R.O.7*. In the tale, Nessie is freed from under a boulder by a frog prince, Frederick. Later, the monster repays the favor by helping Frederick defeat invaders of Britain.

Other films in which Nessie has appeared are *Loch Ness* (1996) starring Ted Danson; *Beneath Loch Ness* (2001); *Monsters, Inc.* (2001); *Scooby-Doo and the Loch Ness Monster* (2004); *Napoleon Dynamite* (2004); *Incident at Loch Ness* (2004); *The Water Horse: Legend of the Deep* (2007); and *Beyond Loch Ness* (2008).

The appearance of the Loch Ness monster in cinema over such a large span of time is a testament to the enduring mystique of the legend. In addition, the ability for the creature to be portrayed in such a wide range of genres, from horror to comedy, shows how versatile the legend is.

TV AND THE MONSTER'S ENDURING POPULARITY

Television is quite appropriate for stories of the Loch Ness monster. Since the legend is burned in the minds of

The Water Horse: Legend of the Deep explores Nessie from a more mythological angle than other films, explaining the beast's origins against the backdrop of a heartwarming family narrative.

most people and since it is a myth that seems to never lose momentum, there are countless ways the myth can be weaved into the brief plots of television storylines.

Take, for instance, a 1971 episode of *Bewitched* called "Samantha and the Loch Ness Monster." The creature is portrayed as a warlock upon whom a spell is cast. In the 1975 *Doctor Who* episode "Terror of the Zygons," the creature is viewed as an alien cyborg that needs to be slain. In these two portrayals, Nessie is portrayed as an evil force that needs to be protected against, which supports humanity's fears about the mystery of the creature.

In lighter portrayals, the British television series *The Family-Ness* showcased the adventures of the monster's family along with their human friends, just as traditional families are portrayed in standard sitcoms. In *The Simpsons* episode, "Money Can't Buy Me Love," the Loch Ness monster is captured and eventually goes to work at a casino.

In one episode of *How I Met Your Mother*, the character of Marshall feels that the "monster" is portrayed unfairly and that it is in fact a gentle creature, spending a week and a half looking for it on his honeymoon. The monster even made an appearance in the 1980s anime series, *Sherlock Hound*. The creature appears at the end of the episode "The Adventure of the Three Students."

Nessie has also appeared in cartoons such as *The Jackie Chan Adventures*, *Spongebob Squarepants*, and *South Park* to great comedic effect. In the *Spongebob Squarepants* episode "Scavenger Pants," Spongebob and Patrick locate the monster by playing bagpipes. The

Scottish music is successful in attracting the traditionally Scottish monster, but Nessie complains upon arriving that it actually hates the sound of bagpipes.

Whether or not Nessie is or has ever been real, the cryptid's impression on the collective consciousness remains. Proving or disproving the monster's existence might yet be a long way off, but the search spurs, for example, the development of sonar technology, which is just one example of how science advances humanity's understanding of the natural world. Mystery, stories, and curiosity motivate people to find out more, to create more, and to share more of the world as it is discovered.

abyss A vast chasm or very deep, seemingly infinite cavity.

bioluminescent The quality of light that is emitted by a living thing.

bovine Related to cows or oxen.

cautionary tale A story with an unfortunate ending that is told in order to warn others of a possible danger.

colossal Exceptionally big or bulky.

cult icon Any entity that gains a dedicated following based on fantastical stories.

cryptid A creature that may or may not exist.

data Information about something being studied.

echosounder A device that locates underwater objects by bouncing sound waves off them.

fallible Capable of being wrong or making mistakes.

fault line A traceable mark on a rock surface that follows a geological rift or split.

formidable Having intimidating qualities that discourage others from approaching or attacking.

herbivore An animal that only eats plants.

Highlands The mountainous area of northern Scotland.

hoax An act performed in order to trick or deceive someone. In cases involving paranormal phenomena, hoaxes are created to fool the public using widely known stories or cryptids.

hypothesis A proposed idea of how data fits together.

kelpie A dangerous horse-shaped water monster in Scottish folklore.

loch The Irish and Scottish Gaelic term for lake.

Loch Ness The third deepest lake in Europe and possibly the home of one or more "monsters."

mirage An optical illusion caused by different atmospheric conditions, commonly produced in the desert or over bodies of water.

multibeam sonar Sonar emitted in a fan shape beneath a ship's hull. It is used to map seabeds.

Nessie Nickname for the Loch Ness monster.

plesiosaur A long-necked aquatic reptile that lived during the time of the dinosaurs. It's been suggested that the Loch Ness monster might be one.

prehistoric Occurring before the age of recorded history.

theory A hypothesis that has been verified by scientific experiments.

thermocline A boundary between water layers of different temperatures.

tully monster Also known as *Tullimonstrum gregarium*, this creature was an invertebrate that lived in shallow tropical waters 300 million years ago.

zoologist A scientist who studies animals.

The Beast of Loch Ness
Public Broadcasting Service
2100 Crystal Drive
Arlington, VA 22202
Website: http://www.pbs.org/wgbh/nova/lochness
Facebook and Twitter: @PBS
The Beast of Loch Ness is a presentation created by the
    PBS show *NOVA* that explores this mysterious creature.

British Columbia Scientific Cryptozoology Club (BCSCC)
8805 Hudson Street, Suite 2305
Vancouver, BC V6P 4M9
Canada
Website: http://www.bcscc.ca/blog
Founded by journalists and scientists, BCSCC is Canada's
    leading cryptozoology organization.

International Cryptozoology Museum
4 Thompsons Point, #106
Portland, ME 04101
Website: http://cryptozoologymuseum.com
Facebook: @cryptozoologymuseum
Twitter: @CryptoLoren
This museum is home to a wide range of exhibits of
    native art, rare zoological specimens, and homages
    to all manner of cryptids, including Nessie.

Loch Ness Discovery Centre
1 Parliament Square
High Street
Edinburgh

EH1 1RE
+44 (0) 131 226 1414
Website: http://www.highlandexperience.com
The Loch Ness Discovery Centre offers information and
tours of lands where the legend exits: Loch Ness,
Inverness, and the Highlands of Scotland.

Loch Ness Exhibition Centre
Drumnadrochit
Loch Ness
Inverness-shire
IV63 6TU
+44 (0) 1456 450573
Website: http://www.lochness.com
The Loch Ness Exhibition Centre informs visitors about
the legend, the people, and the culture of Loch Ness
and its surroundings.

University of British Columbia (UBC)
Okanagan Campus
3333 University Way
Kelowna, BC Canada V1V 1V7
250 807 8000
Website: https://www.ubc.ca
Facebook and Instagram: @universityofbc
Twitter: @UBC
UBC is consistently ranked among the best forty unver-
sities in the world for research and teaching. Their
website has information about Ogopogo, Canada's
version of the Loch Ness monster, as presented by
UBC students at the Okanagan campus.

Bougie, Matt. *Bigfoot, the Loch Ness Monster, and Unexplained Creatures*. New York, NY: Cavendish Square Publishing, 2018.

Dickinson, Greg. *The Rough Guide to Scotland*. London, UK: Rough Guides, 2017.

Garbe, Suzanne. *The Science Behind Wonders of the Water: Exploding Lakes, Ice Circles, and Brinicles*. North Mankato, MN: Capstone Press, 2017.

Lake, G. G. *Take Your Pick of Monster Encounters*. North Mankato, MN: Capstone Press, 2017.

Levete, Sarah. *Fakes and Hoaxes*. New York, NY: Gareth Stevens Publishing, 2017.

Moore Niver, Heather. *Investigating Bigfoot, the Loch Ness Monster, and Other Cryptids* (Understanding the Paranormal). New York, NY: Britannica Educational Publishing, 2017.

Morey, Allan. *12 Terrifying Monsters*. North Mankato, MN: 12-Story Library, 2017.

Nutt, Colin. *Loch Ness*. Broxburn, UK: Lyrical Scotland, 2017.

Peabody, Erin, and Victor Rivas. *The Loch Ness Monster* (Behind the Legend). New York, NY: Little Bee Books, 2017.

Rake, Matthew, and Simon Mendez. *Prehistoric Sea Beasts*. Minneapolis, MN: Hungry Tomato, 2017.

Redfern, Nicholas. *Nessie: Exploring the Supernatural Origins of the Loch Ness Monster*. Woodbury, MN: Llewellyn Publications, 2016.

Woolf, Alex, Bryan Beach, and Andrew Rowland. *The Science of Sea Monsters: Prehistoric Reptiles of the Sea*. New York, NY: Franklin Watts, 2017.

BIBLIOGRAPHY

Adamnan of Iona. *Life of St. Columba*. London, UK: Penguin, 1995.

BBC Newsbeat. "2017 Has Been a 'Record Year' for Sightings of the Loch Ness Monster." BBC, November 15, 2017. http://www.bbc.co.uk/newsbeat/article /41997932/2017-has-been-a-record-year-for-sightings -of-the-loch-ness-monster.

Bord, Janet, Colin Bord, Loren Coleman, and Janet Bord. *Bigfoot Casebook Updated: Sightings and Encounters from 1818 to 2004*. Enumclaw, WA: Pine Winds, 2006.

Childress, David Hatcher. *Yetis, Sasquatch & Hairy Giants*. Kemptom, IL: Adventures Unlimited, 2010.

Darnton, John. "Loch Ness: Fiction Is Stranger Than Truth." *New York Times*, March 20, 1994. https://www .nytimes.com/1994/03/20/weekinreview/loch-ness -fiction-is-stranger-than-truth.html.

Evans, Natalie. "Is the Loch Ness Monster Back? Mysterious Shape Spotted Moving Across Lake After Almost 9 Months Without Sighting." *Mirror*, May 11, 2017. https://www.mirror.co.uk/news/weird-news/loch -ness-monster-back-mysterious-10398013.

Kirkpatrick, Betty. *Nessie: The Legend of the Loch Ness Monster*. Edinburgh, Scotland: Crombie Jardine, 2005.

Kongsberg Maritime. "Creature From the Deep: Kongsberg Maritime Ltd's 'Monster' Discovery." April 13, 2016. https://www.km.kongsberg.com/ks/web/nokbg0238 .nsf/AllWeb/86C5DFECBE7501ECC1257F940037A42F ?OpenDocument.

Martins, Ralph. "Brontosaurus Stomps Back to Claim Its Status as Real Dinosaur." *National Geographic*, April 7, 2015. https://news.nationalgeographic.com/2015

/04/150407-brontosaurus-back-return-apatosaurus
-sauropod-dinosaurs-fossils-paleontology.

McKenzie, Steven. "Film's Lost Nessie Monster Prop
Found in Loch Ness." BBC News Scotland, April 13,
2016. http://www.bbc.com/news/uk-scotland
-highlands-islands-36024638.

Miller, Connie Colwell. *The Loch Ness Monster: The
Unsolved Mystery*. Mankato, MN: Capstone, 2009.

Naish, Darren. "Photos of the Loch Ness Monster, Revis-
ited." *Scientific American*, July 10, 2013. https://blogs
.scientificamerican.com/tetrapod-zoology/photos-of
-the-loch-ness-monster-revisited.

Naone, Erica. "The Nessie Quest." *MIT Technology
Review*, October 15, 2007. https://www
.technologyreview.com/s/408868/the-nessie-quest.

Raynor, Dick. "The Flipper Pictures Re-examined." Loch
Ness Investigation, August 6, 2002. http://www
.lochnessinvestigation.com/flipper.html.

Starr, William W. *Whisky, Kilts, and the Loch Ness Monster: Traveling Through Scotland with Boswell and
Johnson*. Columbia, SC: University of South Caro-
lina, 2011.

Turner, Camilla. "A New Hideaway for the Loch Ness
Monster? Skipper Claims to Have Uncovered Deepest Crevice Yet." *The Telegraph*, January 19, 2016.
https://www.telegraph.co.uk/news/newstopics
/howaboutthat/12108324/A-new-hideaway-for-the
-Loch-Ness-monster-Skipper-uncovers-900-feet-deep
-crevice.html.

INDEX

A

Academy of Applied Sciences, 23, 38
Adamnan, Saint, 7
Amazon Women on the Moon (movie), 50

B

Beaufort Castle, 30
Beneath Loch Ness (movie), 50
Bewitched (TV series), 52
Beyond Loch Ness (movie), 50
Boggart and the Monster, The (book), 47
Boulenger, E. G., 19
buoyancy, 43–44

C

Charteris, Leslie, 47
coelacanth, 16
Columba, Saint, 7
Cooper, Susan, 47

D

Daily Mail, 18, 27
dinosaurs, 12, 26, 40, 43, 45, 48
Dinsdale, Tim, 37
DNA testing, 39
Dr. Who (TV series), 52

E

Edgerton, Harold, 38
Einstein, Albert, 32

F

Family-Ness, The (TV series), 52
Fantastic Beasts and Where to Find Them (book), 47
folklore, 8–9, 47, 48
Fort Augustus, 9, 17, 18, 21, 42
Freddie as F.R.O.7. (movie), 50

G

Gray, Hugh, 21–22
Great Glen, 12, 13

H

hoaxes, 22–23, 29, 50
How I Met Your Mother (TV series), 52
Hydra, 10

I

Ice Age, 12
Incident at Loch Ness (movie), 50
Inverness Courier, 10

61

ABOUT THE AUTHORS

Jenna Vale is a writer from New Jersey for all things paranormal. She has also written or helped write books about ghosts and hauntings, Bigfoot, aliens, and even the Bermuda Triangle.

Martin Delrio is an author living in New York.

PHOTO CREDITS

Cover Michael Rosskothen/Shutterstock.com; pp. 1, 7, 17, 27, 35, 45 (background) sakkmesterke/Shutterstock.com; p. 3 iprostocks /Shutterstock.com; pp. 4–5 (background) Mordolff/E+/Getty Images; p. 5 Bettmann/Getty Images; pp. 8–9 Dusan Kostic/Alamy Stock Photo; p. 11 BlueLotusArt/Shutterstock.com; p. 13 Florilegius/Alamy Stock Photo; p. 15 The Asahi Shimbun/Getty Images; pp. 18–19 Saad Ahmed/EyeEm/Getty Images; p. 22 © Mary Evans Picture Library /The Image Works; p. 25 MichaelTaylor3d/Shutterstock.com; pp. 28–29 Keystone/Hulton Archive/Getty Images; pp. 30–31 Matt Limb OBE/Alamy Stock Photo; p. 34 Westend61 GmbH/Alamy Stock Photo; p. 35 Marevision/age fotostock/Getty Images; p. 39 Rendle Mirrorpix /Newscom; pp. 40–41 Jason Isley-Scubazoo/Science Faction/Getty Images; p. 44 Collection Christophel/Alamy Stock Photo; p. 46 Moviestore collection Ltd/Alamy Stock Photo; p. 49 United Archives GmbH/Alamy Stock Photo; p. 51 Entertainment Pictures/Alamy Stock Photo; cover, back cover, and interior pages (caution pattern) Geschaft/Shutterstock.com.

Design: Michael Moy; Editor: Megan Kellerman; Photo Researcher: Karen Huang